When a Friend Dies

A Book for Teens About Grieving & Healing

Marilyn E. Gootman, Ed.D.

Edited by Pamela Espeland

free spirit
PUBLiSHiNG®

Helping kids
help themselves™
since 1983

Library of Congress Cataloging-in-Publication Data

Gootman, Marilyn E.
  When a friend dies : a book for teens about grieving & healing / Marilyn E. Gootman ; edited by Pamela Espeland.— Rev. and updated ed.
     p. cm.
  Includes index.
  ISBN 1-57542-170-4
  1. Grief in adolescence—Juvenile literature. 2. Bereavement in children—Juvenile literature. 3. Bereavement in adolescence—Juvenile literature. 4. Grief in children—Juvenile literature. 5. Teenagers and death—Juvenile literature. 6. Children and death—Juvenile literature. I. Espeland, Pamela. II. Title.
  BF724.3.G73G66 2005
  155.9'37'0835—dc22

                                                      2005000447

10 9 8 7 6 5 4 3 2 1
Printed in the United States of America

Free Spirit Publishing Inc.
217 Fifth Avenue North, Suite 200
Minneapolis, MN 55401-1299
(612) 338-2068
help4kids@freespirit.com
www.freespirit.com

To my children, Elissa, Jennifer, and Michael

This book was inspired by my love and compassion
for you and your friends. While I cannot protect you
from losses, I hope I can help you through them.

Contents

Foreword

by Michael Stipe, singer/songwriter, R.E.M.

When a Friend Dies is a book about acceptance and compassion. Accepting the sadness, confusion, and pain we experience with loss is as important as healing and moving forward. Showing compassion for yourself is about letting the feelings come and go as they do naturally. There is no right or wrong way to feel when someone dies.

Right now, you may be feeling things you've never felt before—and if you can't understand what you're going through, how could anyone else? No one can completely understand. Everybody hurts in their own way, and your grief and pain are uniquely your own. But feeling lonely and grieving on your own isn't the same as *being* alone. You're not alone.

In this book, other teens share how they felt when their friend died. Reading their words can give you a chance to reflect on your own feelings in a new way. The book's questions and suggestions offer help and reassurance that you can make it through. Be gentle with yourself, take the time you need, and know that the greatest tribute to your friend is just being *you*.

"I just can't believe this happened to one of us." —Seth

"I can't believe she is gone. She was so young and alive." —Erica

"It seems like any minute he should walk into the room. It doesn't seem like he is really gone." —David

"It feels like an alarm clock is supposed to go off soon and this will all be over." —Tanisha

Introduction

Kids are not supposed to die. It's against all the rules of nature. It's not right. It's not fair. It shouldn't ever happen. But it does happen...and when it does, it's scary.

If your friend has died, this book is for you. I hope it will help you to understand what is happening to you and how you can help yourself heal.

When my daughter Elissa was a teenager, one of her friends died. I saw how this death affected my daughter. I spent a lot of time talking with her and being with her, but I also wished there was a book I could give to her. At that time, most books written about death and dying spoke *about* teenagers, not *to* them. As you'll see, this book speaks directly to you.

Some of the words are mine. Some of the words are those of other teenagers whose friends have died, or of famous people who have spoken or written about death. All are meant for you to read at your own pace, in your own time.

You might read this book from cover to cover all at once, starting now. You might read it in little pieces—a page or two today, a paragraph tomorrow, more the day after or next week. How you read it is up to you. But do try to think about the questions, because they will help you to understand what is happening to you. And do try the suggestions—some of them or all of them. They have helped other teenagers, and they may help you, too. You won't know unless you give them a chance.

If you think you need more help, consider talking with a counselor or a therapist. You're going through a lot right now—maybe more than you can handle on your own, or with this book, or with your parents or other family members, caring adults, or close friends. Counselors and therapists are trained to help people through tough times. On pages 98–101, you'll find ideas about where to start looking for this kind of expert help.

You may want to read more books about death and dying. You'll find a list of possibilities on pages 112–113. You can also ask a librarian for ideas, or the media specialist at your school, or your school counselor, or your religious leader, or anyone else whose advice you value and trust.

Bottom line? *You should do whatever works for you.* You have had a terrible shock, and you need to take care of yourself.

This book can be a part of taking care of yourself. Share it with your parents and teachers. They need to know what you are going through, and this book may help them to understand. Especially if you sometimes have trouble putting your feelings into words, this book can speak for you.

Whatever you decide to do—about this book, about your grief, about anything in your life right now—I can promise you one thing: *You will heal with time.* You have probably heard this before. Maybe you don't believe it, but it's true. Not because I say so—because other teenagers say so. They have lived through, learned from, and grown by the horrible experience of having a friend die. You can, too.

Marilyn Gootman
Athens, Georgia

"When my friend died, the rest of the world kept going and no one knew what I was going through. No one could understand the pain I was feeling. I wanted the world to stop and I wanted to just scream out, 'Doesn't anyone realize that I am hurt!' I kept looking at people and thinking, 'You don't have a care, and look at me, one of my friends just died.'" —SELINA

"Things will never be the same." —JACOB

"Will I ever feel okay again?" —TOMAS

How can I stand the pain?

Shock, terror, and disbelief may bombard your body and mind when a friend dies. Surely it must be a mistake! How can it be—alive and breathing one minute, and gone the next?

The pain may seem unbearable. You may fear that your mind is on overload and you might go insane.

D on't panic! You won't always feel this bad. The pain will lessen as time goes on.

After a while, your sad feelings will become fewer and farther between, and your happy feelings will return. Death gashes emotions, just like a knife gashes skin. With time and care, both kinds of wounds heal. They leave scars, but they do heal.

Try to be gentle with yourself. When things start to get unbearably heavy, find a healthy, caring, loving way to distract yourself.

"Gentle time will heal our sorrows."

SOPHOCLES

6

You don't have to do all of your grieving at once.

What activities soothe you and keep your mind occupied when you feel overwhelmed?

It's okay to take your mind off of your grieving for a while. Listen to music, write, draw, exercise....

"I cried hysterically, and then I went numb—kind of like I was watching myself from the outside." —NICOLE

"I can't feel anything. It doesn't feel real." —DEVIN

Why can't
I feel anything?

You may be too stunned to feel anything. You may feel like you're living in a dream.

There is nothing wrong with you. Sometimes peoples' minds shut down when they feel overwhelmed. They shut out the reality of what has happened. This is your mind's way of protecting you from feeling overloaded with pain.

Give yourself some time to let your feelings surface. Then, when they're ready to come out, let them.

"One must go through periods
of numbness that are harder
to bear than grief."

ANNE MORROW LINDBERGH

"The first day back to school was a bitter taste of reality, when you notice the absence. Even after the funeral I still in a way expected her to be there, like it was all a bad dream." —SHANDA

"I've come to realize that grief is something beyond one's control. Something else takes over like an involuntary muscle, working its way through the tragedy." —AMY

How long will this last?

Dealing with death takes time—not just days, but weeks, months, and maybe even years.

You won't be sad and gloomy for the rest of your life. You won't always feel as bad as you do now. Grieving comes and goes. Sometimes you'll feel down, and sometimes you won't.

Nature has a marvelous way of giving your mind and body a break from your hurt once in a while. You may feel sad, then be fine for a few months, then experience sadness and loss again at a later time. This cycle may repeat itself many times during your life.

There's no set schedule for grief. When you feel like grieving, then that is the right time for you. If you let yourself grieve instead of locking your grief inside, the hurt will get smaller and smaller as time goes on. The wound will slowly close up, leaving a healed scar.

Is it wrong to go to parties and have fun?

You have a right and a responsibility to enjoy life and get meaning out of it, even though your friend is gone. While you will have sad times, you are also entitled to laugh and have fun when you are in the mood.

You do not need to feel guilty because you are having fun when your friend is not. Staying sad all the time is not going to help you or your friend.

"You cannot prevent the birds of sorrow from flying over your head, but you can prevent them from building a nest in your hair."

CHINESE PROVERB

What activities do you enjoy?

Do you have any special hobbies?

Is there a hobby or interest you have always wanted to explore?

Maybe now is the time to start.

How should I be acting?

There is no single right way to respond to death. Grief takes many different forms. Each person's grief is unique.

Express your grief in the way that feels most real to you.

Crying

Some people sob and cry. Sadness wells up inside them and pours out.

Some people scream and wail. Maybe that helps them to let out their tension.

Some people stay silent, sometimes crying by themselves, sometimes not.

Just because people are quiet and don't talk about what happened doesn't mean that they aren't hurting. Sometimes people are so shocked or scared that they can't cry. Sometimes they are ashamed of admitting their feelings to others. Sometimes they cry inside.

"Tears are the silent language of grief."

Voltaire

"I'm too scared to cry." —MARIA

"I can't sleep at night. I just keep going over the details in my mind, over and over." —JOEL

Sleeping

Some people go to bed and wake up at their usual times. They get a good night's sleep. Their minds are able to take a break from the pain.

Some people sleep much more than usual. Maybe sleep helps them to escape the pain, or maybe sleep comes because they are so tired from sadness and mourning.

Grieving takes a huge amount of mind and body energy. You can expect to feel tired.

Some people can't sleep at all. Nightmares and scary thoughts keep jumping into their minds. They may not be able to sit still. Maybe moving around helps them to avoid painful thoughts that are more than they can stand.

Going without sleep can make you moodier and more sensitive. It can affect your performance at school and in sports. It can make you look tired and feel irritable. Eventually, it can make you sick.

Try to sleep, even if you don't want to sleep and you're sure that you couldn't possibly sleep. Here are some ideas that might help you sleep:

- Exercise earlier rather than later in the day.

- Relax for an hour or two before going to bed. Read a light, funny book or watch an entertaining TV show or movie. Take a hot shower or bath. Listen to soothing music.

- Avoid caffeine, nicotine, alcohol, and other drugs.

- Cut back on sweets.

- Drink a glass of warm milk. (It includes tryptophan, the same chemical that makes everyone sleepy after a big turkey dinner.)

- Eat a light snack before bed—an apple, a banana, air-popped popcorn, or toast and jam.

Eating

Some people eat like they usually do. Their bodies keep going like always. For them, eating is a habit that doesn't change.

Some people stop eating. The thought of food turns them off. They may vomit when they eat. They may forget to eat. Sometimes their insides are so tied up in knots that it hurts to eat.

Some people overeat. Food, especially sweets and other high-calorie, high-fat junk foods, can seem comforting at times like these.

If you're not hungry, try to eat anyway. The last thing you need right now is to starve yourself. Losing weight because you're too sad to eat is not healthy. Especially during times of stress, you need energy to function.

If you really, truly can't eat a bite, or you can't seem to *stop* eating, talk to an adult you trust.

Have your eating patterns changed?

Think about what you are eating. Try to choose foods that are tasty and are also good for you.

Eating sweets may make you feel better for a short time, but the "sugar crash" that follows will make you feel worse.

Will I be changed?

As time goes on, some people begin to act like they used to. They do not seem to be changed by the experience of having a friend die. They may feel changed on the inside but not show it on the outside.

Some people become silly and giddy. They may joke and fool around a lot because of the tension they feel. They hurt, even if it doesn't look that way.

Some people may become quiet and very sad. They may not want to be cheered up, but they may want to talk.

"I can be changed by what happens to me. I refuse to be reduced by it."

Maya Angelou

Do you think you have changed?
If so, how?

Do you think people are
treating you differently now?

How do you feel when
that happens?

What is "normal"?

All of these different ways of reacting to the death of a friend are "normal."

Don't judge yourself or others by the way you act or the way they act. Pain is pain, no matter how it looks on the outside.

Don't waste your time comparing one person's reactions to another's, or one person's pain to another's. You all hurt, and you all have the right to express it in your own ways.

Before your friend died, you may have thought that all people grieve by crying. Now you know that this isn't true for everyone. Sometimes you can clearly see another person's sadness. Sometimes you can't see it at all. And sometimes people camouflage their true feelings. They may act carefree or boisterous, even though they are hurting inside.

What if I hardly knew the person?

You don't have to be a person's best friend to feel the pain of grief when he or she dies. Even if you just knew *about* the person, you may feel pain. And you may feel pain if you hear about, read about, or watch a television news report about a complete stranger who has died.

You may be reminded of other losses you experienced earlier in your life. You may be frightened by the realization that if this person died, you could die, too. You may have liked or admired the person, even though you didn't know him or her well or at all.

You have the right to your pain. Don't compare it to the pain of someone else who knew the person better. *Pain is pain.*

"I wasn't even there. I didn't even know any of the victims. So why am I so upset?" —MIGUEL

"Sometimes, when I learn about a horrible tragedy, I feel guilty that I'm glad I wasn't there." —JAMIL

When a big disaster or tragedy occurs, thanks to television and the Internet, we are all "there." We are not present in person, but we are "there."

We empathize with others who have lost loved ones. We ache with compassion for them. We feel our own grief and deep sadness for what has happened. We fear that the same thing could happen to us. Suddenly, the world seems like a very unsafe place.

Feeling the pain of others and empathizing with them is a virtue, not a problem. Fearing that the same thing could happen to us is normal, not self-centered.

"The only whole heart is a broken one."

KOTZKER REBBE

Try not to focus on the negative images of tragedy and suffering. Instead, fill your mind with positive images. Think about the courageous, caring people who are helping out. Think about happier times in your own life.

Play with a pet, watch a funny movie, get involved in a project, give yourself a treat, or try some relaxation techniques like taking slow, deep breaths. Make a list of things you've done to get through other difficult situations. Choose one or more to try again.

Protect yourself by limiting your exposure to painful imagery, whether on television or in real-life remnants of the tragedy. Steer your mind to focus on something else.

How can I handle my feelings?

Many thoughts pass through people's minds when they are grieving. These thoughts often trigger strong feelings. Facing and understanding these feelings will help you heal.

"Why did my friend have to die? She was so pretty and smart and nice." —PENNY

"I was sitting in class with her just yesterday. In two years when we graduate, she won't be there." —BETH

Why did my friend have to die?

You may feel like screaming this question out loud to the sky. Maybe your friend died from an illness, or was killed in an accident, or was murdered, or committed suicide. Those are all causes of death, but none answers the question, "Why?"

Different people and different religions have different answers. You may find that one of these answers comforts you. Or you may come up with your own answer. Or you may keep searching for the answer that makes sense to you.

"You don't get to choose how you're going to die. Or when. You can only decide how you're going to live. Now."

JOAN BAEZ

"If only she hadn't gone to pick up her boyfriend at the airport." —Ruth

"If only we had left a few minutes later." —DeShawn

"If only I had taken away his keys." —Andrew

If only...

"If only I had done...."

"If only I had said...."

"If only...."

These are thoughts that torment many people when someone dies. The truth is that awful things happen, and often nobody can stop them.

Death is scary. It makes us feel so powerless. Feeling guilty is a way to avoid feeling powerless. But you are not guilty if your friend has died. It isn't fair to expect yourself to stop another person's death.

"No willpower could prevent someone's dying."

ANNIE DILLARD

If your friend died in an accident or from an illness, then your "if onlys" are your mind's way of helping you feel some control in your life at a very out-of-control time.

If your friend died by suicide, it was your friend's decision, not yours. You are not responsible for that decision. You could not control your friend's thoughts or actions any more than someone else can control yours.

"If only I had been friendlier to her." —TAMIKA

"If I had been there, maybe I could have done something to stop him." —CONNOR

"I never told her how much I cared about her. If only she had known, she might not have killed herself." —FELICIA

Almost all suicide survivors—the people who are still alive after someone they care about commits suicide—blame themselves. But no one is to *blame* for a suicide, not even the person who died. However, that person is *responsible* for his or her own death.

Calling a person responsible is not the same as blaming. It's just stating a fact.

Almost all suicide survivors wonder, "Why did the person choose to leave me?" It's normal to feel abandoned or rejected. When people commit suicide, their primary goal is to end their pain. They do not choose to leave *us*. They choose to leave their pain. They are not thinking rationally.

They may even believe that their loved ones will be better off without them. They are mistaken.

Sometimes it's hard to think of the happy memories when someone commits suicide. Try not to let that final act rob you of your good times together.

Try not to think about how your friend died. Focus instead on how your friend *lived*.

"I wish I had listened to
him. I should have done
something." —TERRELL

"I wish I had told her
not to go." —JESSICA

I wish...

"I wish I had been nicer to my friend...."

"I wish we hadn't argued...."

"I wish I could take back what I said...."

This is another way guilt shows its ugly face. The truth is that arguments, fights, and anger are all part of normal living and feeling. Nobody is perfect, not even the person who died.

> *"Guilt is perhaps the most painful companion of death."*
>
> ELISABETH KÜBLER-ROSS

Life would be very boring if we all tiptoed around each other, afraid to disagree or to be angry because we thought another person might die soon. What went on before has nothing to do with your friend's death.

It is very unlikely that you could have done anything to stop your friend's death. Instead of feeling guilty, try helping another person.

Do something kind and thoughtful for someone else. This is the best way to get back some of the power you have lost.

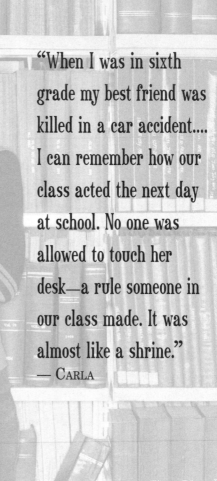

"When I was in sixth grade my best friend was killed in a car accident.... I can remember how our class acted the next day at school. No one was allowed to touch her desk—a rule someone in our class made. It was almost like a shrine."
— CARLA

Sometimes people are afraid to say anything bad about someone who has died. They turn the dead person into a saint.

Every person in this world has strong points and weak points, even those who have died. Loving someone means being honest and accepting the whole person, both the good and the bad, even if the person is dead.

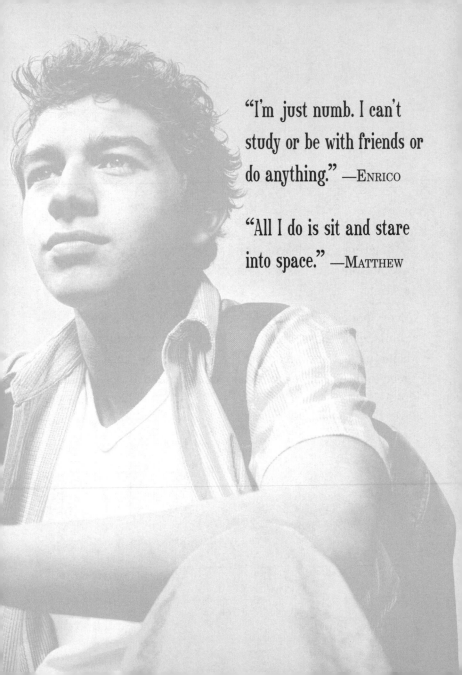

"I'm just numb. I can't study or be with friends or do anything." —ENRICO

"All I do is sit and stare into space." —MATTHEW

I can't think!

The shock of a sudden death makes some people feel as if their minds are frozen. This may be nature's way of protecting your mind so that everything can sink in slowly and you won't be overwhelmed.

If you talk to others and share your sadness, your mind will slowly begin to defrost, and you will start to adjust to your loss.

Sometimes it may seem easier to stay frozen and deny that you are even bothered by what happened. Denying something will not make it go away. Denying your feelings will only keep your pain locked inside where it cannot be healed.

*"Between grief and nothing,
I will take grief."*

WILLIAM FAULKNER

When a friend dies, it has to hurt. Try to admit this to yourself, and talk to someone who will listen and understand.

"First my grandfather died, and then a month later my best friend was accidentally killed. What does God have against me?" —PATRICK

"It's not fair! She didn't deserve to die." —KEISHA

"Everyone says that my friend is in 'a better place.' How the hell do they know?" —LOGAN

"There are so many bad people in the world. She was one of the good ones. Why did she have to die?" —ALEXIS

I'm so angry!

You may feel red-hot anger when a friend dies. You may want to blame someone for your friend's death—another person, your friend's parents, a boyfriend or girlfriend, or God.

You might even be angry at your friend for dying—for being careless, for getting sick, for not wearing a seatbelt, for drinking, for taking his or her own life, or just for leaving you.

You have a right to be angry. It is not fair that your friend has died—not for your friend, and not for you. Go ahead and feel angry. But be careful not to turn your anger onto yourself or others. Be sure to get your anger out in a way that will not hurt anyone.

"Holding on to anger is like grasping a hot coal."

BUDDHA

Run, work out, or go to a place where you can yell at the top of your lungs. Try to think of constructive ways to use the energy from your anger. Build something. Make something.

Do whatever you can to release some of your anger. Most important, talk about it.

Or you can use the energy of your anger to make the world a better place. Here are some ideas:

- Form a Students Against Destructive Decisions chapter at your school. See page 111.

- Start a seatbelt campaign in your school or community.

- Start a hotline for teenagers.

- Do a random act of kindness. See page 110.

- Volunteer to help others. See page 111.

- Do whatever else makes sense to you.

What would help you to release your anger and calm down?

"People are always acting sympathetic and saying they know how I feel, but they don't know how I feel." —Brittany

I feel so alone.

It is normal to feel lonely and left behind after a friend dies. The death has ripped a hole in your life. Your friend is gone, and now it seems as if you must work it out alone.

But you are not alone. Reach out to other people, including those you may not have been friendly with in the past. Try to share your pain. If they knew your friend, they may be suffering, too. By sharing your pain, you will all begin to heal.

Talk to your parents, if you can. If you can't, there are many other adults who can listen—counselors, teachers, other relatives, friends of the family, neighbors, your friends' parents, coaches, youth group leaders, religious or spiritual leaders.

If you know the parents of the person who died, try talking to them. They may appreciate it more than you will ever know.

You may feel alone and left behind, but you are not alone. You have a whole community around you that shares your loss.

"When my best friend was killed, my mom went to the viewing and told me how she looked and I did not want to go. I wanted to remember her alive and beautiful. I did go to the funeral. This was a way for me to realize it was real. I felt like I was there but not really. My mind did not want to accept it. My family did a lot to help me by talking to me." —NICK

Is there someone you would feel comfortable talking to? What about a parent? A teacher? Or another person your age who also knew your friend who died?

Try to approach him or her and begin to chat about anything—the weather, sports, school, a popular movie.... Don't feel as if you have to start talking about your friend's death right away. Let the conversation come around to it. The other person may want to talk about it as much as you do.

Consider joining a support group. A support group is a group of people who share problems and feelings similar to yours. They meet regularly with a counselor or a therapist.

Support groups can be very effective, especially for people who are grieving. Knowing that others are experiencing thoughts and reactions like yours, and being with people who reach out and support each other, can help you heal.

Sometimes support groups are available in schools, especially when a student has died. If your school doesn't offer support groups, check with a counselor or therapist, social worker, or mental health agency. See pages 100–101 for ways to do this. Someone will help you to find a group that is right for you.

I'm afraid to get close to someone else. What if that person dies, too?

The pain of losing a friend can be excruciating. It makes sense to want to avoid ever feeling such pain again. But cutting yourself off from other people because you're afraid of losing them will only make your pain worse by increasing your loneliness.

It is unlikely that another friend will die. Of course, there is no guarantee. But there *is* a guarantee that reaching out to friends can lessen your pain and help you through this difficult time.

> *"If you're going through hell,*
> *just keep going."*
>
> WINSTON CHURCHILL

Needing a friend at this time is a tribute to your friend who died. After all, your friend helped you to realize the importance of friendship.

Look around.
Do you see anybody who might be an interesting friend?

"My best friend was shot and killed. We were best friends since I was four years old. Now I feel angry all the time. I even got mad at a friend who came over to see me. It's like I don't want a friend anymore." —DARYL

If I get close to other people, won't I betray my friend who died?

Some people think that if they make new friends, they are not being loyal to the friend who died. They go out of their way to avoid new friendships.

This doesn't help you, and it doesn't help your friend who died. You can stay loyal to your friend and still reach out to others. Your friend who died will always remain in your heart and in your mind.

> *"Friendship doubles our joy*
> *and divides our grief."*
>
> SWEDISH PROVERB

"We don't feel close like a group anymore. The guys won't come over and be with us." —MARISA

"Some of us want to talk about our friend who died. Some of us don't want to talk about it. We used to get along, but now things are weird." —TYRELL

Some of my friends have changed. I feel like I have lost them, too.

People react in different ways when someone dies. Some may need to break away from painful reminders of the friend they have lost. These "reminders" might include friends they shared in common. Others may be so very sad that they just don't seem the same. Either way, this may feel like another loss to you.

As you open up and talk to people, you may find yourself making new friends and also slowly returning to your old friends.

"After my friend died, I began to worry that my parents would die or that I might die." —CARLOS

"I'm afraid a plane will crash into our house, or a bomb will go off in our town." —ASHLEY

"Every time a car backfires, I think it's a gun." —ANTHONY

I feel afraid all the time.

Sometimes you may feel like you'll go out of your mind thinking about what happened. The fact that death is so final is frightening not just for you, but for all of us. Close your mind down for a while if you have to. Blank out the scary thoughts to give your mind a rest.

It makes sense to be afraid after a sudden, horrifying event like a terrorist attack or a natural disaster, but the odds are in our favor. Although it may not seem that way at the moment, events like these are the exception to the norm.

> *"Death is not the enemy;*
> *living in constant fear of it is."*
>
> NORMAN COUSINS

S ometimes it may be hard to stop thinking about your friend and what happened. Bad thoughts may come into your mind, even when you're enjoying yourself. This happens to many people.

Sometimes people feel guilty about having fun. They think bad thoughts on purpose so they won't enjoy themselves.

"You can clutch the past so tightly to your chest that it leaves your arms too full to embrace the present."

JAN GLIDEWELL

You have a right and a responsibility to live your life and enjoy it.

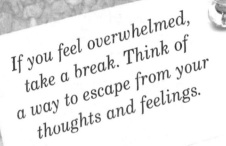

You cannot help your friend by holding yourself back from living your own life to the fullest.

If you feel overwhelmed, take a break. Think of a way to escape from your thoughts and feelings.

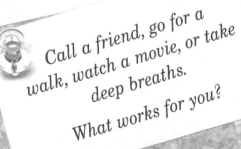

Call a friend, go for a walk, watch a movie, or take deep breaths.

What works for you?

"One minute everything is fine, and a few seconds later I want to break down and cry." —MEGAN

"Every time I hear that song, I'm afraid someone else will die." —JESSE

"In the car on the way to the funeral, my mind became flooded with memories. Slowly at first the scenes appeared in my mind's eye and then built up to frantic speeds. The whole time I sat and stared straight through the windshield while my brain sifted, sorted, filed, and preserved." —ANNA

All of a sudden it hits me, and I get sad.

Sometimes you may find that certain situations—hearing a certain song on the radio, being in a certain place, a change in the weather, words, a smell, a birthday or holiday gathering—remind you of your friend. They may even remind you of when and how your friend died.

You may become very sad, anxious, even panicky. Your heart may start racing and your breathing may speed up. Or your mind may go blank and you may feel numb all over.

This happens to so many people who have lost someone in a sudden, shocking way that it has a special name: post-traumatic stress disorder, or PTSD.

PTSD can take many forms: nightmares, pictures in your mind of your friend's death, flashbacks, fear that someone else close to you will die, painful sadness. You can experience PTSD whenever something reminds you of when and how your friend died.

"Sorrow was like the wind. It came in gusts."

MARJORIE KINNAN RAWLINGS

You're not alone, and you're not crazy! Millions of people experience PTSD. Knowing about it can help you deal with it.

- Practice ways to relax so you can try one the next time you have these feelings. Do some deep breathing or stretching exercises. Tense, then relax every muscle in your body, starting with your head and working down to your toes—or starting with your toes and working up to your head.

- Learn how to meditate.

- Replace unpleasant, frightening thoughts or images with positive ones.

- Get some exercise every day, if you don't already. Walk, run, swim, lift weights—whatever you like to do.

- Talk with an adult you trust. Explain that you're having these feelings whenever you're reminded of your friend's death.

What if nothing seems to work? What if these feelings don't start to fade? What if you just can't seem to get past your friend's death? Then it's time to talk with a doctor or a counselor. See pages 98–101.

When the anniversary of a death comes, you may feel like you did when it first happened. But that doesn't mean you're still in the same place.

You have moved forward, and you won't have to start the whole grieving process again.

"After my friend died, all I could think was, 'Be young, stay young, raise hell while young.'" —ROY

"We're all going to die someday. I know that now for sure. So it doesn't really matter what I do." —JAIME

I'd better enjoy myself as much as I can now, because who knows what tomorrow may bring?

Yes, you should enjoy your life every day. You can do this by living a full life and doing things you enjoy that make you feel worthwhile—things that give your life meaning.

But it is foolish and reckless to do self-destructive things—such as drinking, taking drugs, or driving too fast—because you figure you should enjoy yourself now, while you have the chance.

Why run the risk of destroying your life? If you live a long life, and you probably will, won't this attitude hurt you in the long run?

Some people think that when a friend dies, this reduces the chances that something bad will happen to them. It's as if one death in a group of friends somehow "protects" the other friends from harm.

Statistically, your chances of dying are not any lower—or any higher—now than they were before your friend died. That is why you should still take good care of yourself. Risky behaviors are still risky behaviors.

How many ways can you
have fun without hurting or
endangering yourself or others?

My parents are hovering over me and smothering me.

Most parents want to shield their children from hurt. Few things hurt more than the death of a friend, so it's no wonder that parents are extra attentive or extra protective at times like these.

If your parents are hovering, know that it's because they care. And know that it's okay to wish they would back off! Parents can't protect their children from all the hurt in the world—and they shouldn't try. You need to learn to handle some hurt yourself.

Don't feel guilty about wanting your own space. But tell your parents kindly, without being harsh or rude. Remember that your friend's death has scared them, too. Of course they want to hold you close; the idea that someone could lose a child has become all too real for them. They may be afraid of losing *you*.

Here are some things you may want to tell your parents or other adults (stepparents, guardians, or foster parents) you live with who care for you:

- "I love you, and I know that you love me."

- "I know that you are worried about me because of what has happened."

- "I need to deal with this. Please don't try to protect me."

- "Please don't tell me how to feel."

- "When I talk to you about my feelings, I'd appreciate it if you just listened."

- "Sometimes I might not want to talk to you. I might want to talk to my friends instead. They are going through the same thing I'm going through. We understand each other."

- "Sometimes I may want to talk to another adult I know—a teacher, counselor, or religious leader. This doesn't mean that I'm rejecting you—just that I want to talk to someone who isn't so close to me."

On pages 112–113, you'll find a list of books that can help you better understand what you're going through and why. You may want to share this list with your parents. Maybe they will want to read some of the books, too.

How can I deal with my grief?

Healing any wound, in the body or the mind, takes time. Allow yourself that time. You are entitled to it.

Give yourself permission to grieve. Allow yourself to grieve when and where you need to.

Share your feelings. Write about them. Draw them. Talk to others about your feelings.

Even though you may feel sad when you talk about your friend, talking will help your pain get smaller. Not talking won't make your pain go away. In fact, it may make it stronger. As you force your pain to stay inside, it pushes against you, trying to get out.

That's why it's so important to find someone—a friend or an adult—to talk to. Sharing your feelings with others is a healthy way to release some of your pain.

Sometimes when people don't take time to grieve, they become very angry. Often, they explode at other people and situations that have nothing to do with the death.

Try to think of your emotions inside you as steam inside a pipe. Just as a steam valve slowly releases steam so the pipe won't burst, you can set aside time to slowly grieve so your emotions won't spill out unpredictably and harmfully.

"Give sorrow words; the grief that does not speak Whispers the o'er fraught heart and bids it break."

SHAKESPEARE

If you set aside time to grieve, you will eventually be able to block out your grief at other times. This may be particularly helpful when you really need to concentrate and cannot be distracted, such as during a test. Later, when you are ready, you can come back to your grief.

Remember to live your life to the fullest. Try to think of something positive you learned from your friend, something funny that happened when you were together, or a pleasant time you shared. Know that a part of your friend will always remain with you.

"The pain passes, but the beauty remains."

RENOIR

"When looking back on your lost loved one, try to picture them at their healthiest and happiest." —THERESA

What are your favorite
memories of your friend?

How can I help myself heal?

Share, talk with others, write, draw, listen to music, write music, cuddle with a pet or a stuffed animal, or plant a tree in memory of your friend.

Visit your friend's family. It might be hard to see them, but you can help each other.

Many people find that reaching out to others, doing good deeds, and making the world a better place can help them to heal from the death of a friend.

"The only cure for grief is action."

GEORGE HENRY LEWIS

How can you translate your pain into positive actions that would be a tribute to your friend?

What would be a good way to keep your friend's memory alive—a meaningful memorial to your friend?

What if I can't handle my grief on my own?

Many people who have experienced a great loss find it helpful to speak to someone who has been specially trained to guide people through grieving.

Speaking to a counselor or therapist (psychologist, psychiatrist, or social worker) when you have been hurt by death is no different from going to a medical doctor when you have a deep cut. Both kinds of professionals are trained to help people heal.

Your first visit to a counselor or therapist may be a bit scary and embarrassing. But if the person is in tune with your hurt—if he or she is willing to listen to you and understand your point of view—you will soon feel relieved to have this person to talk to.

If you need to speak to a counselor or a therapist after a friend has died, you are not "sick." You have been injured by events beyond your control, and you are getting help for your injury. It's that simple.

> *"There is no grief like the grief*
> *which does not speak."*
>
> HENRY WADSWORTH LONGFELLOW

What if my friends start acting strange?

Many people who have suffered a sudden, shocking loss could be helped by talking with a counselor or a therapist. In particular, teenagers who are behaving in unusual ways could probably use some guidance. Keep an eye out for friends who:

- drink and/or use other drugs to numb their pain
- stop eating, or eat very little
- eat a lot and force themselves to vomit
- suddenly start doing very poorly in school
- talk about wanting to give up and die
- take self-destructive, even life-threatening risks
- act more aggressive
- act angry at the world
- withdraw from friends and family
- lose interest in things they used to enjoy

Have you noticed any of these behaviors in a friend? If so, speak to a responsible, caring adult—the school counselor, a teacher, your friend's parent, your own parent, a minister, priest, or rabbi. Let that person find help for your friend.

No, you are not betraying your friend. You are being a true, loving friend. The right thing to do—the most caring thing to do—is to tell a responsible, caring adult. You can't solve your friend's problems on your own. That would be an unfair burden for you to carry all by yourself.

Read the list of behaviors on page 95 again. Have you noticed any of them in yourself? If so, please get the help you need and deserve.

> *"Life was meant to be lived....*
> *One must never, for whatever reason,*
> *turn his back on life."*
>
> Eleanor Roosevelt

What adult can you approach to discuss your friend...or yourself?

Who would be a calm, attentive listener?

Who would know where to steer you to get the help you need?

How can I find a counselor or a therapist?

There are many ways to find the help you need for you or a friend. If one way doesn't work for you, try another. Don't give up! Help is available.

Get a personal referral.

Is there someone you know who goes to a counselor or a therapist? If you both feel comfortable talking about it, ask for the name of the counselor or therapist. Ask the person's opinion of the counselor or therapist. Has he or she been helped by the experience?

If you don't know someone who is seeing a counselor or a therapist, ask another person you trust for some suggestions. Good possibilities might include your school counselor, your school psychologist, a teacher, your doctor, or a leader in your faith community.

See about resources in your community.

Following are some ideas you can try. You may want to ask an adult—a parent or other family adult, teacher, or school counselor—to help you, since this process can be intimidating. Just because someone has a title is no guarantee that he or she is the right person for you to see and talk to. An adult can help you to find the right person. He or she should have experience in working with teenagers and/or grief work.

- Look in the paper phone book under "Mental Health Services," "Counselors," "Therapists," "Social Workers," "Psychologists," "Psychiatrists," or "Psychotherapy." If you don't have a paper phone book at home, your local library will have one.

- Look in an online phone directory that covers your city or town. If you don't have a computer at home with an Internet connection, check your local library, community center, or neighborhood coffee shop.

- Type "mental health services" and the name of your city or town in the search window of an Internet search engine like Google or Yahoo.

- Use the Mental Health Services Locator on the National Mental Health Information Center's Web site (www.mentalhealth.org) to find mental health services in your area.

- Call one or more places and ask for a referral. Some help people on a sliding-scale fee basis, which means that you pay only what you can afford.

- Contact one or more of the national organizations listed on pages 106–111 of this book. They will give you the names of counselors or therapists who belong to their organizations and who live in your area.

How can I tell if a counselor or therapist can help me?

You have many choices when it comes to seeking help. School counselors, psychologists, psychiatrists, social workers, psychiatric nurses, certified mental health workers, and pastoral counselors (clergy members) are all qualified to provide therapy. But only *you* can decide whether someone is qualified to be *your* counselor or therapist.

H ere are some questions to ask yourself about someone you are considering:

- Does this person seem to understand my feelings?

- Has he or she experienced the death of someone close? (This isn't essential, but it often helps.)

- Can he or she listen without being judgmental?

- Am I comfortable being honest with him or her?

- Does he or she accept me in a way that helps me to accept myself?

Remember: Counseling or therapy is meant to ease your pain. Only you can tell whether it is working for you. If one person doesn't seem to be helping, try someone else. Keep trying until you find someone who is right for you.

Will I ever be okay again?

At first, when a friend dies, it's hard to imagine how life can go on...but it does. It's hard to imagine that things will ever go back to normal, or almost normal...but they will.

I wish that this had never happened to you and your friend, but it did. There is nothing you can do to change what has happened, but there is much you can do to help yourself.

I have gone through what you are going through now. I know other young people whose friends have died. I can make this promise: You will grow from this tragedy. You will learn more about yourself and others. You will become more sensitive. Your view of the world will change.

"I still miss those I loved who are no longer with me, but I find I am grateful for having loved them. The gratitude has finally conquered the loss."

RITA MAE BROWN

No one would ever choose to grow because of the death of a friend. But now that it has happened to you, what can you do to make meaning out of your experience? Think about that in the weeks, months, and years ahead. You will find a way.

Meanwhile, you may take some comfort in the words of others who have spoken or written about death. Go back and read the quotations by famous people—Sophocles, Anne Morrow Lindbergh, and others—found throughout this book. If there is one that is especially inspiring or helpful to you, write it down on a piece of paper and carry it in your wallet or calendar. Or create your own quotation. Share your words with a friend who is also grieving. Help each other.

Resources

American Association of Suicidology (AAS)
4201 Connecticut Avenue, NW, Suite 408
Washington, DC 20008
(202) 237-2280
info@suicidology.org
www.suicidology.org

The American Association of Suicidology works to understand and prevent suicide. Call to find a crisis center in your area. On the Web, click on "Support Groups" to find a support group in your area for suicide survivors. Download *SOS: A Handbook for Survivors of Suicide,* a booklet packed with helpful information.

American Foundation for Suicide Prevention
120 Wall Street, 22nd Floor
New York, NY 10005
1-888-333-AFSP (2377)
inquiry@afsp.org
www.afsp.org
For teens: www.afsp.org/education/teen/index.htm

The American Foundation for Suicide Prevention is dedicated to advancing knowledge about suicide and the ability to prevent it. They provide information and education about depression and suicide. Their Web site for teens includes a resource guide and TV/radio public service announcements.

American Psychiatric Association (APA)
1000 Wilson Boulevard, Suite 1825
Arlington, VA 22209
(703) 907-7300
apa@psych.org
www.psych.org

A psychiatrist is a medical doctor who is trained to help
people with emotional problems. If you are looking for a
psychiatrist, you can go to the APA's Web site and click on
"district branches and state associations." Then click on "district branch directory." Scroll down to find the district branch
in your state. People there can give you names and phone
numbers of psychiatrists in your area.

American Psychological Association (APA)
750 First Street, NE
Washington, DC 20002
1-800-374-2721
www.apa.org

A psychologist is a counselor who usually has received a doc-
toral degree from a university. Call 1-800-964-2000 to get a
referral to a psychologist in the United States or Canada. If
you live elsewhere, you can contact your national psychological association or a local mental health facility.

The Bright Side—Wings of Support
www.the-bright-side.org

This Web site provides support for anyone who is feeling emotionally overwhelmed by life.

The Dougy Center for Grieving Children & Families
P.O. Box 86852
Portland, OR 97286
1-866-775-5683
help@dougy.org
www.dougy.org

The Dougy Center runs the National Center for Grieving Children & Families, which provides support and training locally, nationally, and internationally to individuals and organizations seeking to assist grieving children, teens, young, adults, and their families. Contact them to learn about groups in your area. Check out the "Help for Teens" pages on their Web site.

National Association of Social Workers (NASW)
750 First Street, NE, Suite 700
Washington, DC 20002
(202) 408-8600
www.socialworkers.org

A clinical social worker has received advanced education and training to help people deal with emotional problems. On the Web site, click on "find a social worker" to locate one or more in your area.

National Board for Certified Counselors and Affiliates (NBCC)
3 Terrace Way, Suite D
Greensboro, NC 27403
(336) 547-0607
nbcc@nbcc.org
www.nbcc.org

NBCC maintains a registry of people who hold an advanced degree with a major study in counseling and who have met national standards developed by counselors. To find a certified counselor, go to their Web site and click on "counselorfind."

National Hopeline Network
1-800-784-2433

For people in crisis who need immediate help. Trained telephone counselors are available 24 hours a day, 7 days a week.

National Mental Health Consumers' Self-Help Clearinghouse
1211 Chestnut Street, Suite 1207
Philadelphia, PA 19107
1-800-553-4539
info@mhselfhelp.org
mhselfhelp.org

The Clearinghouse helps connect individuals to self-help and advocacy resources and offers expertise to self-help groups and other peer-run services for mental health consumers.

Network for Good
8615 Westwood Center Drive, Suite 1A
Vienna, VA 22182
(703) 265-3683
www.networkforgood.org

This nonprofit organization uses the Web to help people get more involved in their communities—from volunteering and donating money, to getting involved with issues they care about.

The Random Acts of Kindness Foundation
1727 Tremont Place
Denver, CO 80202
1-800-660-2811
rakinfo@actsofkindness.org
www.actsofkindness.org

This foundation inspires people to practice kindness and to "pass it on" to others. They provide free educational and community ideas, guidance, and other resources to kindness participants through their Web site.

SAMHSA's National Mental Health Information Center
P.O. Box 42557
Washington, DC 20015
1-800-789-2647
www.mentalhealth.org

Information Center staff members are skilled at listening and responding to questions from the public and professionals.

The staff quickly directs callers to federal, state, and local organizations dedicated to treating and preventing mental illness. On the Web site, click on the "Services Locator" to find information about mental health services in your state.

Students Against Destructive Decisions (SADD)
P.O. Box 800
Marlborough, MA 01752
1-877-SADD-INC (1-877-723-3462)
info@sadd.org
www.sadd.org

Students Against Destructive Decisions (SADD), formerly known as Students Against Driving Drunk, can provide you with information about how to start a SADD chapter in your school. They can also help you make an action plan for activities and programs dealing with underage drinking, other drug use, impaired driving, and other destructive decisions.

Volunteer Match
volunteermatch.org

One way to heal yourself is by helping others. This Web site encourages visitors to "Get out. Do good." Enter your ZIP code and press "Search" for a list of volunteer opportunities in your area. Check out the ones marked "T" for Teens.

Recommended reading

Healing Your Grieving Heart for Teens: 100 Practical Ideas by Alan D. Wolfelt, Ph.D. (Fort Collins, CO: Companion Press, 2001). A grief counselor offers compassionate suggestions for dealing with the scary, often uncontrollable emotions that come up after you've lost someone.

The Healing Your Grieving Heart Journal for Teens by Alan D. Wolfelt, Ph.D. (Fort Collins, CO: Companion Press, 2002). Open-ended, thought-provoking questions help you to write and heal. Some encourage you to write about what you miss about the person who died, difficult feelings you're having, or things you wish you had done or said before the death.

I Will Remember You: What to Do When Someone You Love Dies: A Guidebook Through Grief for Teens by Laura Dower (New York: Scholastic Paperbacks, 2001). Thoughts and quotations from famous people (Emily Dickinson, Dr. Seuss, E.B. White, Mother Teresa, and others), personal stories from real teens, and creative exercises help you move through your pain and sorrow.

A Teen's Simple Guide to Grief by Alexis Cunningham (Carson, CA: Jalmar Press, 2001). The sadness and depression that come with grief can be overwhelming. This short, simple book offers suggestions for daily steps that can help you feel better.

When Will I Stop Hurting? Teens, Loss, and Grief by Edward Myers (Lanham, MD: Scarecrow Press, 2004). Stories from teens who have lost a family member, advice for reaching out to others, encouragement to help you through the grieving process, and warning signs for when grief leads to depression.

For adults

Bereaved Children and Teens: A Support Guide for Parents and Professionals by Earl A. Grollman (Boston: Beacon Press, 1996). Articles and reflections by 14 writers explore topics including terminal illness, cultural and religious responses to death, death education in schools, and using film and drama to teach about death.

Helping Teens Cope with Death by The Dougy Center for Grieving Children and Families (Portland, OR: The Dougy Center, 1999). The Dougy Center for Grieving Children and Families is internationally renowned for its peer support groups and training efforts to help young people recover from loss. This book details the unique experience of teen grief and offers ways for caring adults to support adolescents throughout the grieving process.

Index

About the author

Marilyn E. Gootman, Ed.D., is founder of Gootman Education Associates, an educational consulting company that provides workshops and seminars for parents and educators focusing on successful strategies for raising and teaching children.

Dr. Gootman has been in the teaching profession for over 25 years, and her teaching experiences range from elementary school to the university level. The author of numerous books and articles, she is know nationally for her advocacy efforts on behalf of children, parents, and teachers. Her media appearances include CNN and other major networks, as well as radio and television broadcasts throughout the United States and Canada.

Harold Alan Photographs/Hal Schroeder

Marilyn and her husband, Elliot, are the parents of three grown children.

Other Great Books from Free Spirit

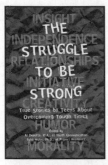

Fast, Friendly, and Easy to Use

www.freespirit.com

Our Web site makes it easy to find the positive, reliable resources you need to empower teens and kids of all ages.

The Catalog.
Start browsing with just one click.

Beyond the Home Page.
Information and extras such as links and downloads.

The Search Box.
Find anything superfast.

Your Voice.
See testimonials from customers like you.

Request the Catalog.
Browse our catalog on paper, too!

The Nitty-Gritty.
Toll-free numbers, online ordering information, and more.

The 411.
News, reviews, awards, and special events.

 Our Web site is a secure commerce site. All of the personal information you enter at our site—including your name, address, and credit card number—is secure. So you can order with confidence when you order online from Free Spirit!